The Mystery of the

MAMMOTH BONES

And How It Was Solved

ALSO BY JAMES CROSS GIBLIN

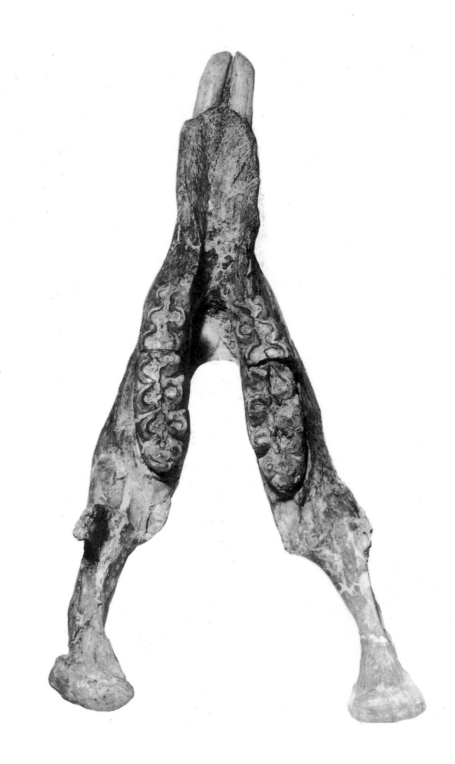

JAMES CROSS GIBLIN

The Mystery of the
MAMMOTH
BONES

And How It Was Solved

HARPERCOLLINS*PUBLISHERS*

Acknowledgments

Thanks are owed to the following institutions for their help in providing research material
and illustrations for this book:

Department of Library Services, The American Museum of Natural History
Department of Geology, Paleontology & Mineralogy, Hessisches Landesmuseum, Darmstadt, Germany
National Portrait Gallery, Smithsonian Institution
The New-York Historical Society
The New York Public Library
The Pennsylvania Academy of the Fine Arts

Special thanks to Scott DeHaven, Assistant Manuscripts Librarian, American Philosophical Society,
for his assistance and suggestions.

FRONTISPIECE PHOTO: The creature's jawbone with teeth, as viewed from above.
Neg. No. 311395, photo by E. M. Fulda, courtesy Dept. of Library Services,
American Museum of Natural History

Library of Congress Cataloging-in-Publication Data
Giblin, James.
 The mystery of the mammoth bones : and how it was solved / James Cross Giblin.
  p.   cm.
 Includes bibliographical references (p.   –   ) and index.
 Summary: Describes the efforts of the artist, museum curator, and self-taught paleontologist, Charles Willson Peale,
to excavate, study, and display the bones of a prehistoric creature that is later named "mastodon."
 ISBN 0-06-027493-X. — ISBN 0-06-027494-8 (lib. bdg.)
 1. Mastodon—New York (State)—Newburgh—Juvenile literature.   2. Peale, Charles Willson, 1741–1827—
Juvenile literature.   3. Paleontologists—United States—Biography.   [1. Mastodon.   2. Peale, Charles Willson,
1741–1827.   3. Paleontologists.]   I. Title.
QE882.U7G48   1999   98-6701
569'.67—dc21   CIP
                                                                                                          AC

Typography by Al Cetta
1 2 3 4 5 6 7 8 9 10
❖
First Edition

For William C. Morris,

children's book promoter

extraordinaire

Contents

The Mystery of the
MAMMOTH BONES

And How It Was Solved

CHAPTER 1

News of the Bones

Less than two hundred years ago, no one knew that creatures like the dinosaurs had ever roamed the Earth. No dinosaur fossils had yet been discovered. But an American artist and scientist, Charles Willson Peale, was about to unearth the fossilized skeleton of another giant creature from the prehistoric past.

Peale's discovery would help to pave the way for the later identification of the first dinosaur fossils. It would also lead people to question how long there had been life on the Earth, and the age of the Earth itself. However, Charles Willson Peale had no inkling of what lay in store for him, and the world of science, when he sat down to read his mail on a spring morning in 1801.

One letter in particular caught Peale's eye. It came from a friend in New York State, and enclosed with it was a clipping from a Newburgh, New York, newspaper. The clipping described a number of mysterious fossil bones that had been found in a marshy field near Newburgh. His friend thought Peale would be interested in the bones because they were unusually large and appeared to be extremely old.

Self-portrait of Charles Willson Peale in uniform, 1777–78.
Courtesy American Philosophical Society

Peale certainly was interested. Although he had no formal scientific training, he had immersed himself in the study of animals and plants and, fifteen years earlier, had founded the first natural history museum in America. It was housed in rooms Peale rented at the American Philosophical Society in Philadelphia, his home city.

Thousands of people, young and old, visited Peale's museum each year. They gazed in wonder at stuffed examples of snakes and pheasants, deer and wildcats, set against backdrops that resembled the creatures' natural habitats. Learning how to pre-serve the specimens on display was "a work so difficult," Peale once said, "that had I known what I was about to undertake, I would perhaps have rather put my hands into the fire. But such is the bewildering study of Nature, that it expands the mind to embrace object after object. . . ."

As he became more and more involved with his museum, Peale put aside his former career as an artist who specialized in painting portraits. Now he devoted much of his time to reading about the latest scientific discoveries throughout the world, and to corresponding with scientists in France and England as well as the United States. And he was always on the lookout for new attractions—"curiosities," he called them—that would draw even bigger crowds to his museum.

That was why Peale was so intrigued by the newspaper clipping from Newburgh. If he could obtain the bones of the creature described in the article and put them on display, he was sure, they would create a sensation. According to the description, the animal must have been almost as big as an elephant. Its remains were so big, in fact, that the writer of the article called it a mammoth.

This was not the first time Peale had heard of a mammoth. Twenty years earlier, when he was known mainly as an artist, he had been asked to draw the fossilized bones of a mammoth that had been discovered at Big Bone Lick in what is now Kentucky, near the Ohio River.

Fossils are the hardened remains of ancient animal or plant life that have been preserved for thousands of years in the Earth's crust. Most fossils are formed by a process known as *petrifaction*. In this process, which takes a very long time, the normal cells of the animal or plant are gradually replaced with mineral deposits that turn the cells to stone. The most favorable conditions for petrifaction occur in the sediments at the bottom of the sea, and in bogs and swamps like those at Big Bone Lick.

The huge mammoth fossils from Kentucky fascinated Peale and made him want to know more about the mysterious creature. He read everything he could find on the subject,

North American mammoth, painting by Charles R. Knight.

Neg. No. 328179, *photo by Logan, courtesy Dept. of Library Services, American Museum of Natural History*

beginning with reports of the discovery of mammoth bones in Siberia in the far north of Russia early in the eighteenth century. It was Russian scientists who gave the creature its name, which comes from the biblical word *behemoth*, meaning "huge animal." But no one in Russia had found any living examples of the beast.

Peale also read about the vast hoard of mammoth fossils that had been unearthed in Kentucky starting in the 1740s. These had probably been formed when the mammoths came to places like Big Bone Lick for the salt deposits there and were either trapped in quicksand or drowned. Over the course of centuries, their bones became petrified. A few of these fossils, including the ones Peale had drawn, remained in the American colonies. The majority were shipped by French and English explorers to their home countries, where they were studied carefully by scientists.

These European experts put forth two different theories about the bones. Some thought they came from a known animal, such as an elephant or hippopotamus. Others said they must come from an animal that had not yet been discovered—a "great *incognitum*" ("unknown") now living in some remote, unexplored corner of the Earth.

A Native American tradition seemed to support the second theory. It said that long, long ago, a herd of the huge creatures came to Big Bone Lick and began to destroy all the deer, elk, and buffalo that had gathered there. When the Great Man who lived above saw what was happening, he became enraged. The god descended to the Earth, seated himself on a neighboring mountain, and hurled his lightning bolts into the herd of invading mammoths.

All the fearsome creatures were killed except for one giant

bull. Ignoring a wound in his side, the bull sprang over the Ohio River and the Great Lakes and raced away to the north. According to the Native American tradition, he still lived and ruled in that icy region.

Neither theory could be proved, however, on the basis of the scattered bones that had been discovered thus far. Only a complete, or almost complete, skeleton of the mammoth would enable scientists to make exact comparisons with the skeletons of elephants and other large mammals. That was another reason, besides the possibility of obtaining a unique exhibit for his museum, why Charles Willson Peale was thrilled by the newspaper clipping and the letter from his friend. For if the bones found in Newburgh were as numerous as the clipping indicated, there might be enough to assemble a skeleton of the mammoth.

Part of the unknown animal's lower jaw, with teeth.

Neg. No. 311057, photo by E. M. Fulda, courtesy Dept. of Library Services, American Museum of Natural History

What a marvelous contribution to science that would be!

The clipping said that a farmer named John Masten had unearthed the bones while digging a pit on his property. Masten realized at once that the fossils were unusual. He piled them up in a corner of his granary and offered to show them to anyone who was interested. Peale's friend thought the scientist might want to make a trip to Newburgh, sixty-seven miles up the Hudson River from New York City, to see the bones for himself.

Peale was elated when he put the letter and clipping aside. Of course he wanted to see the bones! The self-taught scientist had turned sixty that spring, but he possessed the energy and enthusiasm of a much younger man. And nothing excited him as much as a fresh challenge—especially one that involved his scientific interests. After arranging for one of his sons to look after his museum while he was away, Peale made plans to leave for Newburgh as soon as possible.

CHAPTER 2

Sailing Up the Hudson

Today, if the traffic isn't too bad, one can drive the 160-mile distance between Philadelphia, Pennsylvania, and Newburgh, New York, in under three hours. But in Charles Willson Peale's time, the trip was a major undertaking. First, he loaded his trunk onto an express stagecoach that took a day and a half just to get to New York City, with an overnight stop along the way. From New York, he would have to book passage on a boat that sailed up the Hudson River to Newburgh.

New York in June 1801 was not the great metropolis we know now. With fewer than 50,000 inhabitants, it ranked second in size to Philadelphia, then the largest city in the United States and the new nation's capital. Peale planned to spend several days visiting friends in New York before continuing his journey to Newburgh. He also hoped to gather more information about the giant bones.

His plans got a boost when he went to see a professor of natural history and chemistry at Columbia College, then situated at Park Place, near the present City Hall. The professor had

The New Jersey Palisades along the Hudson River,
as sketched by Charles Willson Peale.
Courtesy American Philosophical Society

published a detailed article about the mammoth bones and was glad to share his knowledge with Peale. He also gave Peale a letter of introduction to a doctor in Newburgh, James Graham, who had been present when most of the bones were excavated.

Peale reserved a place on a sloop that was scheduled to sail up the Hudson on June eighteenth. But lack of a favorable wind kept it at the dock until the nineteenth. In 1801, almost all ships, large and small, depended on the wind for their power. It wasn't until 1807 that the inventor Robert Fulton launched the first successful steamship.

As the sloop sailed north, Peale got out his sketchbook and

made ink drawings of the steep New Jersey Palisades and other dramatic sights along the Hudson. Although Peale as an artist was best known for his portraits of George Washington, Benjamin Franklin, and other famous men, he had a strong response to landscapes also. He wrote in his diary:

> We had a charming passage to West Point & the scenes presented every moment were grand; all on the great scale. I was enchanted with the sight of such stupendous mountains, the grander part of which were covered with woods and here & there projecting a huge rock. But in some places we see almost perpendicular walls of them, with trees and shrubbery growing from their crevices—and sometimes dripping water besprinkling the front. . . .

Peale did not comment on the age of the cliffs, but today we know that rock layers like the ones he observed are millions, if not billions, of years old. Geologists estimate the age of the planet Earth at 4.6 billion years, and speculate that the beginnings of life on the Earth occurred as early as 4.2 billion years ago. In Peale's day, however, even scientists were limited in their estimates of the Earth's age. These scientists still believed, along with most people, that God had created the Earth and everything on it in a relatively short time.

In 1650, an Irish bishop, James Ussher, had announced that the Creation must have occurred in 4004 B.C. He had arrived at this figure by a careful calculation of all the names and dates mentioned in the Old Testament. Thus, according to Ussher, life had existed on earth for less than six thousand years.

Most Europeans in Ussher's time saw no reason to disbelieve

his calculations. These people relied on the Bible to be their guide in everything. But many European scientists did question the bishop's dates. They had found the fossils of conch and oyster shells in rocks high in the mountains, and guessed that over the centuries the Earth had changed drastically. What was once soft had become hard and solid, and what was once at the bottom of the sea had somehow risen to the highest mountain peaks. Could all this have happened, as Ussher said, in just six thousand years?

New discoveries in the eighteenth century raised fresh questions about Ussher's estimate. Geologists studying rock formations in Germany and England determined that different layers of rock represented different periods in the Earth's history. The most recent layers were those closest to the surface, while older layers were found deeper down. The geologists also realized that the various layers could be identified by the distinctive fossils contained within each one. The more the geologists learned, the harder it became to fit their discoveries into a six-thousand-year time frame.

As they examined the fossils from different rock layers, the geologists faced another major problem. The Bible, in Ecclesiastes 3:14, says, "I know that, whatsoever God doeth, it shall be for ever: nothing can be put to it, nor any thing taken from it. . . ." But some of the fossils the geologists unearthed resembled no known living creatures. Was it possible that these bones came from animals that were now extinct? If so, how could their extinction be reconciled with the teachings of the Bible?

In 1801, the pioneering French paleontologist Georges Cuvier expressed his thoughts on animal extinction. Paleontology is the branch of geology that deals with prehistoric forms of life

The French scientist Georges Cuvier, with his decorations.
Neg. No. 28000, courtesy Dept. of Library Services, American Museum of Natural History

through the study of plant and animal fossils. It was a new science when Cuvier began his work in the 1790s. Cuvier did not challenge the Bible directly. He simply said that nothing in paleontology was more important than to "discover if the animal species which existed in the past have been destroyed, or if they have merely been modified in their form, or if they have been transported from one climate to another."

The year Cuvier wrote these words—1801—was the same year in which Charles Willson Peale set out to investigate the mysterious mammoth bones. Peale had heard of Cuvier, but it's unlikely he had read the French scientist's article about extinction. Nor is it likely that Cuvier was aware of Peale's mission. But whether they knew it or not, both scientists were in pursuit of the same goal.

The closer Peale got to Newburgh, the more eager he was to see the giant bones. At last, on the afternoon of June twenty-second, the boat let him off on the east side of the Hudson River, directly across from Newburgh. Peale spent the night with friends at Fort Putnam, a Revolutionary War stronghold, and the next day he was

View from the lower end of Newburgh, New York, looking down the Hudson River. *Watercolor by Charles Willson Peale.*
Courtesy American Philosophical Society

ferried across the Hudson on a barge. No bridges spanned the mighty river then.

Peale went at once to the house of Dr. Graham, armed with the letter of introduction he had been given in New York. Graham was a friend of John Masten, the farmer on whose property the bones had been discovered. The doctor received Peale warmly and, at Peale's urging, told him how the bones had been unearthed.

Masten's farm abounded in marl pits, or morasses. Under a top layer of turf, these watery pits contained layers of marl, a crumbly soil that makes a good fertilizer. One day, Masten's son thrust his spade into a marl pit and struck what he thought was a log. But when he dug it out, he saw to his astonishment that it was a large bone. He measured the bone and found that it was three feet nine inches long and had a circumference of eighteen inches at the smallest point. From its shape, he guessed it was a thighbone.

The young man alerted his father and the other farmworkers, and they continued to dig. By evening several other bones had been discovered. Word of the unusual finds spread throughout the neighborhood, and the next day more than a hundred people, including Dr. Graham, joined the search.

The diggers uncovered a large number of additional bones, but in their haste to bring them out of the pit, many of the fossils were damaged. The hips, tusks, and skull of the creature were all broken when chains pulled by oxen were used to try to yank them free of the clay and marl.

Suddenly, water from underground springs burst through the bottom of the pit. The diggers fought it with bowls, buckets, and milk pails, but the flood proved to be too much for them. By the fourth day, the water level in the pit had risen so high that the workers realized they had no hope of continuing to dig. Reluctantly, they abandoned their effort, even though they were convinced that many more bones remained in the depths of the pit.

When Dr. Graham finished his story, it was too late for Peale to go to Masten's farm that day. But the doctor offered to take him first thing in the morning. The two men rode the four miles to the farm in Graham's horse-drawn carriage. After the doctor had explained the purpose of their visit, Masten led him and Peale to the granary, where the mammoth bones were stored.

Peale gazed in awe at the mass of fossilized bones. Spread out on the floor were the neck bones, most of the vertebrae from the animal's spine, and some from its tail. Most of the ribs were there, too, but many of them were broken. Near the ribs lay bones from the creature's hips, legs, and feet; fragments of its head; and a five-foot-long piece of one of its great, curving tusks.

Missing were some of the back and tail bones, the breast bone, and the animal's jawbone and skull. One whole tusk and part of the other were missing also. If these bones could be found, there would be almost enough to construct a complete skeleton of the mammoth.

After Peale had caught his breath, he asked John Masten if he could make drawings of the

Side view of one of the mysterious animal's tusks.
Neg. No. 5619, courtesy Dept. of Library Services, American Museum of Natural History

bones. The farmer agreed, and Peale set to work at once, using large sheets of paper he had brought with him from New York. Dr. Graham took his leave, after arranging to return later in the day for the artist.

When lunchtime came, Masten invited Peale to eat with him and his family. During the meal of ham, lettuce salad, rye bread, and cold spring water, the farmer's eldest son suddenly asked Peale if he was interested in buying the bones.

Peale had hoped for just such an opportunity, but was surprised it had come up so quickly. He told those at the table that he would definitely be interested in acquiring the bones, provided the price was not too high. Turning to Masten, he asked the farmer how much he wanted for them.

The farmer seemed unwilling to name a price, so Peale decided to be completely straightforward. He told Masten he was prepared to pay $200 for the bones that had already been dug up, and $100 more for the right to excavate those remaining in the pit.

Masten hesitated before replying, then said that Peale's offer seemed low. He had been told the bones were very valuable; couldn't Peale afford to pay more for them?

No, Peale answered, he could not pay any higher price.

Masten said nothing more about the matter, and Peale feared the farmer's silence meant there would be no deal. After the meal was over, the artist went back to drawing the bones. He still had not finished by the time Dr. Graham arrived to pick him up.

Before he left to spend the night at the doctor's, Peale told Masten he would return in the morning to complete his drawings. He asked the farmer to think again about his offer for the bones. The farmer said nothing in response, merely nodded his head in a vague way.

Peale couldn't decide whether the farmer's gesture meant a "yes" or a "no." As he rode away from Masten's farm with Dr. Graham, he didn't feel hopeful about his chances of obtaining the bones. He consoled himself with the thought that at least he'd have detailed drawings of them.

CHAPTER 3

Getting Ready to Dig

When Peale returned to Masten's place the next day, the farmer was at work in the fields. Peale took this to mean Masten had decided not to accept his offer. With a sigh, he reached for his pencil and began to draw another one of the bones. But when Masten came into the granary a little later, he surprised Peale by saying he was ready to sell.

The artist thought quickly. He told Masten he would give him $50 in cash and arrange to have the balance of $150 paid later. That was fine with the farmer, but he asked for one thing more: Peale's expensive-looking double-barreled gun. Peale replied that the gun had been a gift, and he could not bear to part with it. However, he promised to send Masten a similar gun from New York, and the farmer agreed to that arrangement.

With the sale concluded, Peale asked to see the marl pit where the bones had been found. Masten led him across the fields and down a slope to the pit. Later, Peale expressed his feelings at that moment in a letter to a friend. "My pleasure was so great while viewing the great pond where the bones were dug

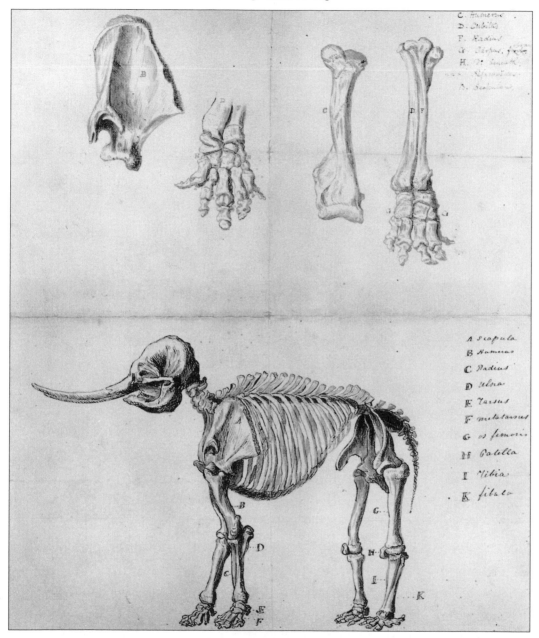

Working sketch of the mysterious creature's skeleton and some of its leg
and foot bones, drawn by Peale's artist son Rembrandt Peale.

Courtesy American Philosophical Society

up that I had an urge to dive into it at once to search for more."

Once he got over that impulse, Peale took a more realistic look at the situation. "The pit is now full of water, at least twelve feet deep—and it appears an Herculean task to explore the bottom where the remainder of the bones are supposed to lie," he wrote. "But I can assure you that I have not the least doubt of completing the skeleton without breaking a single bone."

He knew, though, that he would need to make careful plans for the excavation, bearing in mind all the difficulties that must be overcome. Otherwise, he would have no chance of achieving his goal.

As they left the pond, Masten offered to take Peale and the bones he had bought to Newburgh. There the artist could book passage on the next boat for New York. They loaded the bones into the farmer's biggest wagon and set off without delay. At Newburgh, Peale had the fossils packed in large wooden barrels—all except for the thighbone and several others that were too long to fit.

Before departing, Peale assured Masten that he would return as soon as he'd raised the funds for the second excavation and had assembled all the necessary equipment. At that point, he'd be able to pay Masten the rest of the money he owed him.

The news of Peale's unusual purchase spread quickly after he arrived in New York. More than eighty prominent people, including Aaron Burr, the vice-president of the United States, came to the house where the artist was staying. They were eager to see the four-foot-long thighbone and the other unpacked fossils.

After a few days in New York, Peale made arrangements to have the fossils shipped by boat to Philadelphia while he himself returned to his home city by stagecoach. Once there, he planned to put the bones together so that he'd have a better idea of which ones were missing. He told a friend how he planned to go about it. "I am preparing to erect this skeleton in my parlor, which is the only room I can use, but I am apprehensive it—although large—will not be of sufficient size (26 feet long and 15 feet high). If the tusks cannot get enough room within, I contemplate extending them through the end window and building round them on the outside. . . ."

He had agreed to postpone his attempt to unearth the rest of the bones until after Masten had harvested his crops. The farmer feared the plants might be trampled by curious onlookers. While he waited, Peale mended the broken bones in his collection and began to fit them together. He also started to gather funds for the excavation. After he showed his drawings of the bones at the American Philosophical Society, its board of directors granted him a loan of $500 to cover his basic expenses.

Peale also wrote for help to his friend Thomas Jefferson, who had recently been elected president of the United States. Jefferson, like Peale, was interested in science and had written about the mammoth in his book *Notes on the State of Virginia*, published in 1787. In it, he reported that some European scientists thought the creature was an elephant because of its tusks, while others thought it must be a hippopotamus because of the shape of its teeth.

Jefferson himself believed it was neither animal. He wrote: "Naturalists acknowledge that the tusks are much larger than those of an elephant, and the grinders [teeth] many times greater than those of the hippopotamus, and essentially different in form." Therefore, he concluded, the tusks and teeth found in

Kentucky, Siberia, and other places must have come from some other huge animal that no longer lived in those locales.

Jefferson responded enthusiastically to Peale's request for help in excavating the mammoth fossils. If Peale could assemble a complete skeleton of the animal, it should prove once and for all that the mammoth was a unique creature. To demonstrate his support, Jefferson said he was arranging for the navy to lend Peale one of its pumps for use in the excavation. He had also asked the Army to provide the artist with a couple of sturdy tents.

With his loan from the Philosophical Society, and the promise of President Jefferson's assistance, Peale left for New York to buy supplies for the expedition. Accompanying him was his artist son Rembrandt, who would be his chief assistant. Twenty-two-year-old Rembrandt Peale had been named for the famous Dutch artist Rembrandt van Rijn.

In New York, Peale was able to borrow a pump immediately from the shipping company whose boat he had taken on his first trip to Newburgh. That meant he would not have to wait for the navy's pump to arrive. The boat's captain also helped him and Rembrandt acquire the rope, blocks, and other gear they would need for the excavation. The next evening, just as the sun was setting, the two Peales boarded the boat for the journey up the Hudson. All their supplies were stored safely belowdecks.

As they sailed slowly north in the gathering darkness, Peale—like many travelers before and since—admired the lights of New York City. The city's streets had been illuminated since 1762, when an ordinance required oil-burning lampposts to be put up on every corner. "The effect was beautiful," Peale wrote in his diary. "In addition to the lamps of the streets, the quantity of lights from the bottom to the tops of many houses heightened the brilliancy of the scene. . . ."

There were so many passengers on board the boat that all the berths were filled. Many of the travelers preferred to lie down on the tops of chests. Peale spread out a small tent from his baggage and slept on deck. The folded tent made a rather hard bed, he wrote, but it was more comfortable than sleeping two in a berth.

Arriving in Newburgh, Peale and his son set about obtaining lumber for the excavation. They also hired twenty-five local men and boys to help with the work. At Masten's farm, the workmen built a watertight cofferdam of wooden planks around the edge of the pit to help keep the sides from caving in. Peale scouted the surrounding area and decided the best place to put the water removed from the pit was a natural hollow about sixty feet away.

The borrowed pump was not powerful enough to get the water out of the pit by itself. To supplement the pump, Peale designed a wheel-and-bucket mechanism. It was similar to draining devices that had been in use since the days of ancient Rome. A rotating chain of buckets hung over the pit from a wooden tripod. The chain was connected to a large wooden wheel, twenty feet in diameter and wide enough for three or four men to stand abreast in it. As the men walked, the wheel turned and the chain lifted the buckets out of the water.

When the buckets reached the highest point on the chain, they tipped over. The water they held spilled into a trough that carried it downhill to the hollow. Meanwhile, other buckets were constantly filling with more water from the pit below. By the second day, the water level had dropped so low that the workmen were able to start digging for fossils.

First, they had to remove one to two feet of peat or turf. When it was gone, they dug through a two-foot layer of what

Peale's rough drawing of the wheel-and-bucket device
used to drain the water from Masten's morass.

Courtesy American Philosophical Society

farmers called yellow marl—vegetable matter intertwined with thick, yellowish roots. Below that came another two-foot layer of gray marl, which resembled wet ashes. Finally, the diggers reached a layer of decayed seashells that farmers called white or shell marl. Most of the mammoth bones were buried in the layers of gray and white marl. The best-preserved ones came from deepest down, where no air had been able to get to them over the centuries.

Hundreds of people flocked to Masten's farm in carriages and wagons to watch the digging operation. They gazed in awe at the giant wheel, and some of them volunteered to help turn it. Encouraged by all the attention they were getting, the workmen began to show off. When one of them unearthed an especially large bone, he'd wave it around for everyone in the crowd to see.

Within a week, though, the crowd's cheers turned to groans as trouble developed on the worksite. The sides of the pit, weakened by the removal of so much mud and water, began to slant inward. At the same time, the layer of marl at the bottom of the pit started to rise, pressed upward by underground springs. And ice-cold water from the springs kept on seeping into the pit.

The workmen struggled to reinforce the sides and drain the water from the bottom. They also continued to dig. Over the next few days, they discovered parts of the mammoth's breastbone and hip bone and another section of a tusk. But the creature's skull and jawbone were not among the finds. Peale reasoned that they must have sunk deeper into the pit.

Unfortunately, the workmen could not search for these bones. Despite the men's efforts to prop them up, the walls of the pit were now slanting more steeply than ever. They threatened to fall in at any moment, trapping whoever was working in the pit at the time. Besides that danger, the springwater in the pit was so cold that the men could not stay in it for more than a few minutes at a stretch.

The workmen were willing to keep on going, but Peale and his son realized it would be futile to continue the dig. The forces of nature were too powerful to resist. Reluctantly, the workmen took down the wheel and lowered the chain and buckets. They loaded the equipment on wagons, along with the bones they had gathered. The crowd went home, and the Peales prepared to depart also.

But they were not ready to give up their quest for mammoth bones. Dr. Graham had told the elder Peale of another morass eleven miles away, on land owned by a Captain Joseph Barber. Workmen had found four ribs from a mammoth while digging a pit in Barber's morass some years before.

After getting permission from Captain Barber, Peale went to see the pit on his property. It was much smaller than the one at Masten's farm, but even so Peale decided it was worth exploring. Who could tell? Perhaps it contained the bones Peale needed to complete a mammoth skeleton.

CHAPTER 4

In Search of a Jawbone

Peale and his son, together with their hired hands, spent almost a week digging a ditch to drain the second morass. The hot August sun beat down on them all day long, and a thick screen of trees around the site kept any cooling breeze from reaching them. But the workers didn't seem to mind the heat. They were happy to be making $1.12 a day, which was considered an excellent wage at the time.

At week's end, the water level in the morass was low enough for the men to begin digging for bones. In the next few days they unearthed four of a mammoth's teeth, a few vertebrae from its back and tail, some toe bones, a broken shoulder blade, and a complete set of the creature's ribs. But they found nothing from the mammoth's head except for the teeth and its two tusks, both of which were badly decayed. There was no sign of the animal's skull . . . or its jawbone.

Without the latter two elements, Peale would not know what a mammoth's head had looked like, and thus would be unable to construct a complete skeleton of the creature. He had little hope of unearthing an intact skull, since the bones in it were probably too fragile to have survived. But a jawbone was sturdier, and would give him most of the dimensions he needed for the head. That's why it was so important to find a jawbone.

Under Peale's direction, the workers stored the bones they had excavated from Barber's morass in a shed near the pit. They were careful to keep these fossils separate from the ones found earlier on Masten's farm. When he had enough bones to assemble a skeleton of the mammoth, Peale wanted to be able to identify where each of the various parts had come from.

The workers kept on digging until they had explored the entire bottom of the morass. They turned up nothing more of value, however. Peale hated to admit defeat, but he decided it would be a waste of time and money to dig further in this location. He paid off his laborers, and they went away satisfied while Peale and his son pondered where to turn next.

Fortunately, there were in the vicinity several other morasses in which a few mammoth bones had been found. We now know that these swampy areas were left behind after the glaciers of the last Ice Age retreated to the north. The fertile vegetation surrounding the morasses probably attracted migrating mammoths. But at the center of the morasses there were often treacherous limestone sinkholes. When a heavy, lumbering mammoth stepped into one of these sinkholes, it was likely to become trapped. Millennia later, its fossilized bones would be found, preserved in the very pits of marl and limestone that had killed the creature.

First, the Peales mounted their rented horses and rode to the farm of Alexander Colden. According to local lore, Colden had unearthed some mammoth teeth and a patch of the animal's

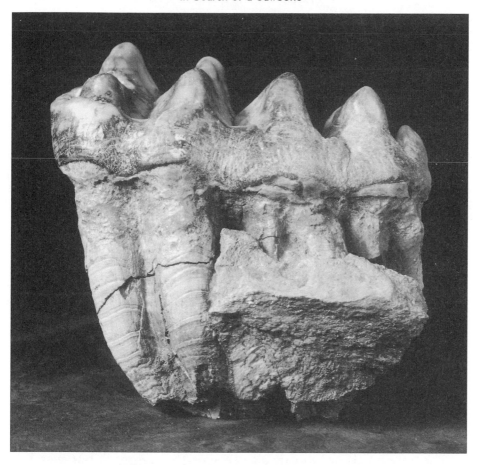

Side view of a fossilized tooth from the creature.

Neg. No. 316088, photo by Julius Kirschner, courtesy Dept. of Library Services, American Museum of Natural History

grayish-brown hair from a morass on his property. Colden led the Peales to the marshy area, which was quite large but only five feet deep. He told the Peales he would be glad to have a ditchdigger explore the center of the morass in a search for more bones.

The Peales thanked Colden for his offer, but they weren't hopeful about the results of the excavation. It wasn't likely that many of the creature's bones would have survived in such a shallow morass—especially not large ones like the jawbone the Peales were seeking.

That afternoon Peale and his son rode on to a farm that had formerly belonged to the Reverend Robert Annan. It was Annan who, twenty years before, had discovered the first mammoth bones in the area while digging a drainage ditch for a swamp. He had shown his finds to General George Washington when the general was encamped nearby during the Revolutionary War.

Later in the war, Annan also showed the bones to Dr. Christian Michaelis, a German physician who was in the service of the British army. Michaelis had a great interest in paleontology, and after the war he arranged to return to Annan's farm to dig for more bones. Unfortunately, one heavy rain after another prevented the German from completing his work. Annan gave him some of the bones found earlier so that he would not return home empty-handed, and Michaelis donated them to a museum in the German city of Kassel.

The weather was fine when Peale and his son arrived at the old Annan place, but Peale was disappointed to find that much of the morass there had dried up over the years. What was left was no more than four feet deep and had a very hard bottom. Peale got permission from the farm's present owner to dig at the deepest spot, but decided not to start work right away. He was even less hopeful of success here than he had been on the Colden farm.

Now there was only one more place on the Peales' list of possible digging sites: Peter Milspaw's farm in a remote, thinly settled area twenty miles west of the Hudson River. The Peales had heard that farmer Milspaw, several years earlier, had dug up a number of mammoth bones on his property. So they loaded their pump, tackle, buckets, and other equipment into a borrowed wagon and set out for Milspaw's farm over a double row of hills.

Rembrandt Peale described in an essay what happened when they got to the farm. "From his log hut, Peter Milspaw accompanied us to the edge of the morass, which was surrounded by a fence to keep Milspaw's cattle out. Here we fastened our horses, and followed our guide into the center of the morass, or rather marshy forest, where every step was taken on rotten timber and the spreading roots of tall trees. Breathless silence reigned here amid unhealthy fogs, and nothing was heard but the fearful crash of some moldering branch or towering beech tree.

"The holes dug to obtain manure [fertilizer], out of which a few bones had been taken six or seven years before, were full of water, and connected to other holes containing an even greater amount. To empty one hole, we would have to empty them all," Rembrandt wrote.

Yet he and his father could tell from looking at the morass that it might be large enough and deep enough to contain the bones they were looking for. "And so, since we had already conquered so many difficulties, my father and I resolved to embrace the only opportunity that now offered the prospect of further discovery," Rembrandt added.

With fresh energy, the Peales hired a few workers from the area and got ready to drain the ponds in the morass. They set up the pump and erected scaffolding for their buckets, as they had done on the Masten farm. Then they built a series of wooden troughs to conduct the water through a mass of tangled tree roots and away from the morass.

By the middle of the following afternoon, almost all the ponds had been drained. Now the workers would be able to dig on every side from the spot where the first discovery of the bones had been made. To celebrate, Peale and his son hosted a picnic supper that evening and invited the workers and their friends. The guests ate freshly baked bread and smoked ham, and washed the meal down with generous amounts of grog—rum diluted with water. Everyone was in a good mood by the time the sun set, and eleven of the men agreed to come back the next day to help with the excavation.

Working steadily, the men unearthed a small but well-preserved collection of bones. Among them were some of a mammoth's ribs, a kneecap, one of the creature's heel bones, and several toe bones. But they did not find the jawbone the Peales would need in order to construct a complete and accurate skeleton of the creature.

The next day the men branched out from the site of the original pit, hoping to locate another hoard of bones. They excavated a considerable quantity of marl with their picks and shovels, but turned up only a few new fossils. Peale and his son were close to despair. If this search failed to produce the desired results, where could they turn next? They had no idea. Still, it seemed pointless to continue digging if nothing more was likely to come of it. They were about to call a halt when one of the workmen suddenly gave a shout.

The man had been poking into the soft ground about eighty feet from the Peales with a long, pointed stick. By this means, he had learned how to distinguish harder objects that were buried beneath the surface. Now his stick had struck something solid, and it seemed to be quite big. Excited, both Peales joined the man, and Rembrandt grabbed his stick. After a few more exploratory pokes, Rembrandt announced that the object was a bone . . . and there was more than one.

All the workers hurried to the spot, and soon they had cleared the ground of plants and shrubs. Next, they cut the sod into squares and tossed the squares to one side. As they dug deeper into the earth and got closer to the bones, the elder Peale warned the men to go slowly with their spades. If they weren't careful, they might damage the fossils.

At last they uncovered the first of the fossils, a complete though very fragile shoulder bone. Beneath it they found one of the mammoth's thighbones, and the inner and outer bones of a foreleg. And then, after clearing away more of the moldy soil, they came upon the bone the Peales had been seeking from the start of the expedition—an under jaw in almost perfect condition.

The creature's jawbone with teeth, as viewed from above.
Neg. No. 311395, photo by E. M. Fulda, courtesy Dept. of Library Services, American Museum of Natural History

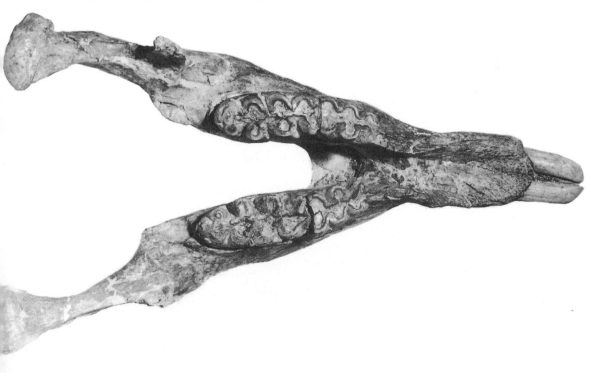

When the workers lifted out the huge bone, everyone cheered. "Gracious God, what a jaw!" the elder Peale exclaimed. "How many animals do you suppose have been crushed between it!"

The discovery of the jawbone seemed to crown all of the artist's labors. As far as he knew, it was the only one that had been found complete anywhere in the world. But there were still more fossils to be unearthed from this treasure trove. Restraining his excitement, Peale urged the workers to press on.

CHAPTER 5

The Mammoth Takes Shape

The workers continued to probe with the pointed stick and soon made another startling discovery. It was the upper part of the mammoth's skull.

Unfortunately, the bones in it had decayed to such an extent that the men were unable to remove the skull in one piece from the marl. Most of it broke into small fragments as soon as it was touched. But Peale and his son got a good sense of the skull's overall shape before it crumbled into dust. This would help them to reconstruct the skull later from wood when they assembled the mammoth's skeleton.

Having located the jawbone and the remains of the skull, Peale decided there was no point in digging further at Milspaw's place. They had found everything they had been seeking there. And as a result of their various excavations in the area, they had gathered more than enough bones to construct not one but two mammoth skeletons!

Thus ended what Rembrandt Peale called "our strange and laborious campaign of three months." He and his father, with the

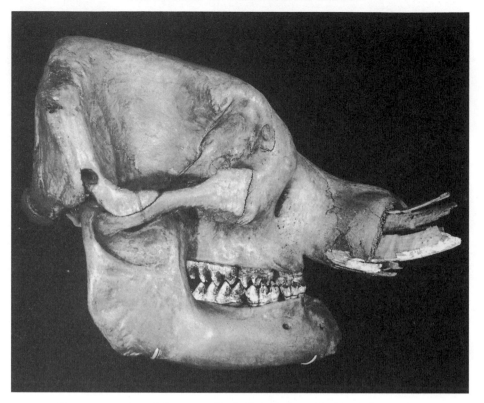

Reconstruction of the animal's skull including the base of its tusks.
Neg. No. 35445, photo by Thomson, courtesy Dept. of Library Services, American Museum of Natural History

aid of the hired workers, packed all the bones into four large crates. They made sure that the finds from the two most success-ful digs, at the Masten and Milspaw farms, were kept separate. This would make it easier to assemble the two skeletons, and would also help to ensure their accuracy.

The Peales loaded the crates and their other baggage onto two wagons and rented a third to carry the pump. Then they set off for Newburgh, and a boat that would carry them and their precious cargo to New York City. There Peale opened one crate of bones and displayed the contents to hundreds of the city's residents who lined up to see them. The visitors gasped at the sight of the huge under jaw, which alone weighed more than sixty pounds.

Some people thought Peale was making a mistake by showing a portion of the bones before he had assembled them into a skeleton. But the artist was convinced this preview would only whet the viewers' interest. Then they would want to travel to Philadelphia to see the complete skeleton when it went on exhibit.

Peale was afraid to send the bones to Philadelphia by boat, for fear they would be lost if the vessel sank. So he arranged to have the four cases go by stagecoach, even though it was much more expensive. He and Rembrandt made the trip by boat, accompanied by their less valuable luggage.

Once the Peales and their finds had arrived safely in Philadelphia, it took three months to construct two complete mammoth skeletons from the bones. The job was much too complicated to be done in Peale's home. Instead, he closed his museum temporarily, and he and Rembrandt used the space to put the skeletons together. Assisting them were several laborers who moved the heavy bones around and raised them into position.

Peale and his son also had the help of Dr. Caspar Wistar, a well-known Philadelphia physician and scientist. Wistar had studied the anatomy and bone structure of elephants, which were quite similar to those of the mammoth. Because of his knowledge, he could give the Peales useful advice as to where the various bones should go in the two mammoth skeletons. Wistar was especially helpful in determining how to arrange the small bones in the creatures' feet.

After the Peales had settled on the placement of the bones, a prominent sculptor, William Rush, showed them how to fasten the fossils together with plaster of Paris and wire. He also helped the Peales to fill in the gaps in the skeletons. For example, the under jaw found at the Milspaw farm was inserted in the first skeleton. But it also served as a model for a wooden duplicate that was included in the second skeleton.

Peale and his son painted red lines around the artificial bones in the skeletons to indicate that they were not the real thing. All the artificial bones were carved as accurately as possible, however, and only the top of the head and the tip of the tail were missing from both skeletons.

Assembling the skeletons was "a long and arduous task," according to the elder Peale, for no one knew exactly what the completed animals should look like. "Yet the novelty of the subject, the producing of the form, and as it would seem a second creation, was delightful. And every day's work brought its own pleasure."

As the skeletons gradually took shape, even the Peales were stunned by their tremendous size. One of the mammoths was slightly bigger than the other. The bigger animal's length, from its chin to its rump, measured fifteen feet. It stood eleven feet tall from its shoulders to the bottoms of its feet. The curving tusks alone were ten feet long, and according to Peale the entire skeleton weighed more than a thousand pounds. To give even greater emphasis to its bulk, he decided to set the skeleton of a tiny mouse next to the mammoth when it went on display.

At last, in late December 1801, Charles Willson Peale announced that the bigger skeleton was ready for viewing. The exhibition opened to the general public on December twenty-fifth. Christmas was not widely celebrated in the early 1800s, so

One of the two skeletons assembled by the Peales.

Courtesy Hessisches Landesmuseum, Darmstadt

Skeleton of the Mammoth

IS NOW TO BE SEEN
At the Museum, in a separate Room.

FOR ADMITTANCE TO WHICH, 50 CENTS; TO THE MUSEUM,
AS USUAL, 25 CENTS.

*Of this Animal, it is said the following is a Tradition, as delivered in
the very terms of a Shawanee Indian:*

" TEN THOUSAND MOONS AGO, when nought but gloomy forests covered this land of the sleeping Sun, long before the pale men, with thunder and
fire at their command, rushed on the wings of the wind to ruin this garden of
nature----------when nought but the untamed wanderers of the woods, and men as
unrestrained as they, were the lords of the soil-----a race of animals were in being,
huge as the frowning Precipice, cruel as the bloody Panther, swift as the descend-
ing Eagle, and terrible as the Angel of Night.   The Pines crashed beneath their
feet; and the Lake shrunk when they slaked their thirst; the forceful Javelin in
vain was hurled, and the barbed arrow fell harmless from their side.   Forests were
laid waste at a meal, the groans of expiring Animals were every where heard;
and whole Villages, inhabited by men, were destroyed in a moment.   The cry of
universal distress extended even to the region of Peace in the West, and the Good
Spirit interposed to save the unhappy.   The forked Lightning gleamed all around,
and loudest Thunder rocked the Globe.   The Bolts of Heaven were hurled upon
the cruel Destroyers alone, and the mountains echoed with the bellowings of death.
All were killed except one male, the fiercest of the race, and him even the artillery
of the skies assailed in vain.   He ascended the bluest summit which shades the
source of the Monongahela, and roaring aloud, bid defiance to every vengeance.
The red Lightning scorched the lofty firs, and rived the knotty oaks, but only
glanced upon the enraged Monster. At length, maddened with fury, he leaped over
the waves of the west at a bound, and this moment reigns the uncontrouled Monarch
of the Wilderness in despite of even Omnipotence itself."

[*Carey's Museum, December,* 1790,—*page* 284.]

Ninety years have elapsed since the first remains of this Animal were found
in this country----they were then thought to be the remains of a GIANT: Numerous have been the attempts of scientific characters of all nations, to procure a
satisfactory collection of bones; at length the subscriber has accomplished this
great object, and now announces that he is in possession of a SKELETON of this
ANTIQUE WONDER of North America; after a long, laborious and uncertain enterprize.
They were dug up in Ulster county, (State of New York) where they must have
lain *certainly* many hundred years-------no other vestige remains of these animals;
nothing but a confused tradition among the natives of our country, which states
their existence, *ten thousand Moons ago ;* but, whatever might have been the ap-
pearance of this ENORMOUS QUADRUPED when clothed with flesh, his massy bones
can alone lead us to imagine; already convinced that he was the LARGEST of
Terrestial Beings!   C. W. PEALE.

NB. *The Mammoth and Museum will be exhibited by lamp light, every evening,
(Sunday evenings excepted) until* 10 *o'Clock.*

[*Printed by John Ormrod.*]

Advertisement for the opening of the exhibit of the skeleton at the Peale Museum.

Courtesy American Philosophical Society

hundreds of Philadelphians, young and old, flocked to Peale's museum on the twenty-fifth to see the mammoth. Thousands more visited the museum in the weeks and months that followed. To accommodate the crowds, Peale kept the museum open by the light of oil lamps until ten P.M. every day except Sunday.

The regular admission charge to the museum was 25 cents, but Peale charged 50 cents extra to view the mammoth, which was exhibited in a separate room. When some visitors grumbled, he explained that the additional fee was necessary because "the expense of this undertaking has been so great." Peale estimated that the costs of purchasing the bones, making the expeditions to New York, and mounting the skeletons came to $2,000—a very large sum at the time.

As news of the mammoth exhibit spread throughout the new nation, Americans quickly added the word *mammoth* to their vocabularies. They used it as an adjective to describe anything that was extra large. Newspapers reported on a mammoth peach tree, a mammoth bird, and a mammoth pudding. There was even an account of "a mammoth egg-eater [human] who swallowed 42 eggs in ten minutes, together with the shells."

Charles Willson Peale could have relaxed and basked in the triumph of his exhibit if he'd wanted to. Instead, he made even more ambitious plans for the second mammoth skeleton that he and Rembrandt had constructed. Rembrandt had long wanted to see the artworks in the great museums of England and continental Europe. For his part, Peale wanted European scientists to have an opportunity to view the mammoth. He had sent plaster casts of a few of its bones and teeth to Georges Cuvier in France, but that was not the same as viewing the entire skeleton.

Peale thought he saw a way to accomplish both goals. Why

not have Rembrandt and his younger brother Rubens take the second mammoth skeleton on a tour of London, Paris, and other European cities? They could charge a fee to view the skeleton, as Peale had in Philadelphia, and use the income to pay their travel expenses. Rembrandt and Rubens would have a chance to study art, and they would also gain valuable business experience from managing the exhibit.

Above all, European scientists would be able to see the mammoth firsthand. They could compare its bone structure with the various types of elephants that were on display in European museums and zoos. They could also compare the skeleton with the remains of the mammoths discovered earlier in Siberia. Was the American mammoth the same animal, or was it a different creature altogether? And was it still living, or was it extinct?

Rembrandt and Rubens were excited by the prospects of the European trip. The night before they took apart the second mammoth skeleton in order to pack it, Rembrandt hosted a dinner party under the animal's massive rib cage. Thirteen gentlemen sat comfortably around a small table and a portable piano. Among the guests were William Rush, the sculptor who had helped to put the skeletons together, and Dr. William Stephen Jacobs, a well-known chemist.

Before they started to eat, the guests raised their glasses in honor of the Peales and their great accomplishment. Here are a few of the toasts they offered:

"To All Honest Men—If they cannot feast in the *Breast of a Mammoth*, may their own breast be large enough."

"To the American People—May they be as pre-eminent among the nations of the earth as the canopy we sit beneath surpasses the little mouse."

"To the arts and sciences—Nursed in a genial soil, and fostered with tender care, may their honor prove as *durable* as the *bower* which surrounds us."

The guests ended by toasting Rembrandt and Rubens, and wishing them every success on their trip to Europe.

CHAPTER 6

A New Name for the Mammoth

Before leaving for England, Rembrandt and Rubens exhibited the second mammoth skeleton in the ballroom of a New York City hotel. Rembrandt thought this would be a good way to raise additional funds for their trip, and he was right. He and Rubens kept the exhibit open from nine A.M. to nine P.M., and within two months, more than 3,000 New Yorkers came to see the giant beast.

The brothers encountered only one serious problem with the exhibit. Skeptical New Yorkers doubted whether the mammoth's ten-foot tusks could have been that long in real life. Feeding their doubts was the fact that both of the tusks on display in New York were substitutes made of wood. To convince future viewers, Rembrandt wrote his father and asked him for one of the actual tusks from the Philadelphia skeleton. Peale sent it at once.

The Peales were scheduled to sail for England between the fourteenth and seventeenth of June, 1802, but bad weather over the Atlantic delayed their departure. They finally left New York in mid-July. When they arrived in London, they were dismayed to find that the prices for everything except clothing were much higher than in America. The room they rented for six months to exhibit the mammoth cost the huge (for that time) sum of £150—about $666.

The room was in an excellent location, however. It was just a few doors away from the residence of the Prince of Wales, in a fashionable neighborhood known for its coffeehouses and sweet shops. Rembrandt was sure this location would help the exhibit to draw large crowds of well-to-do visitors. They could view the mammoth, a creature unlike any that had been seen in London before, and then enjoy a cup of coffee or a pastry in one of the nearby restaurants.

Rembrandt and Rubens erected the skeleton by the end of September 1802 and "exposed it to public view" on October 4. The Peales spared no expense to make Londoners aware of the exhibit. They hired men to put up posters on blank walls and carry announcements about the streets on square boards. The Peales also took out small but expensive advertisements in the major London newspapers. A typical ad read as follows:

> The very extraordinary Skeleton of the Mammoth, a species of Gigantic animal which is not known to exist, and which was lately dug up in America, is now Exhibiting at No. 118, Pall-Mall, where it has been visited by Ladies and Gentlemen of the first respectability, all of whom have expressed the highest satisfaction. This skeleton is eleven feet high, and fifteen feet long, with bones of an astonishing bulk. From its teeth it must have fed on flesh, and could not but have been a terror to the country where it lived. . . .

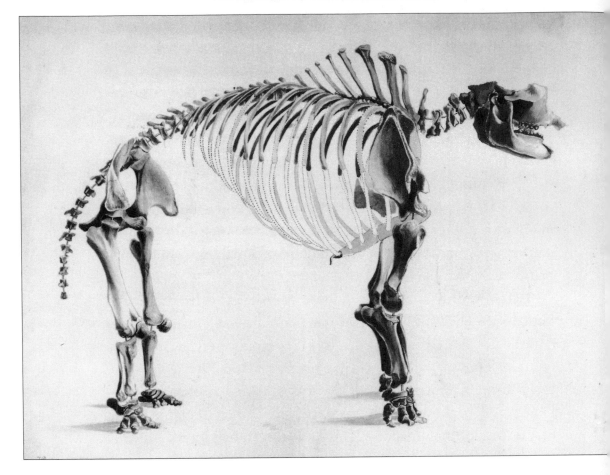

Drawing by Rembrandt Peale of the actual bones in the second skeleton.
Courtesy American Philosophical Society

Despite these publicity efforts, the exhibit did not attract the expected crowds. It took in only the equivalent of $43 the first week, $87.50 the second. In a letter to his father, Rubens guessed that the poor attendance was due to the fact that the English did not like Americans because of the Revolution. To counteract this, friends advised the Peales to stop mentioning in their ads that the bones were from America.

Rembrandt and Rubens followed this advice, but still the crowds did not come. In another letter, Rubens wished they were back home with the skeleton, for he was sure they would make more money exhibiting it in America. "Here we pay so dear for everything, the expenses run away with the profits," he moaned.

But Rembrandt was determined to transform the London exhibit into a success. Hoping to establish the importance of the mammoth, he wrote a long essay in which he told how he and his father had discovered and assembled the two skeletons of the creature. He went on to compare the mammoth's skeleton with the skeleton of an elephant, and came to the conclusion that they were entirely different animals.

There were especially striking differences in their teeth, he wrote. Whereas the elephant's teeth were suitable for eating leaves, ground plants, and other vegetation, the teeth of the mammoth were much larger and resembled those of the hippopotamus. The mammoth's teeth also had unusual domelike projections on their tops, and they were completely covered with a thick coat of enamel like the teeth of carnivorous animals. From this, Rembrandt decided that the mammoth must have been a meat eater. Since its remains had been found in watery morasses, he thought it probably had lived near lakes and rivers and fed on small animals and fish.

He noted that there were also major differences between the mammoth's tusks and the tusks of an elephant. Elephant tusks were short in relation to the animal's size and nearly straight. But the mammoth's tusks curved in a great spiral, reaching an overall length of almost eleven feet.

Rembrandt recalled that when he and his father assembled the mammoth skeletons, they weren't sure how to place the

Oil portrait of Rembrandt Peale by his father, Charles Willson Peale, 1818.
Courtesy National Portrait Gallery, Smithsonian Institution

tusks. The sockets showed that the tusks grew out in a forward direction, but did not indicate whether they curved upward or downward. Rembrandt decided they would have served no useful purpose if they had curved upward. But if they pointed downward, the mammoth could have used them to root up shellfish or as an aid in climbing a riverbank. So he placed the tusks in a downward position on the two skeletons.

Rembrandt ended his essay about the mammoth by taking a

strong stand on the question of extinction. He knew he would be attacked by those who believed that everything God had created was still alive somewhere on the Earth. But he couldn't deny the evidence to the contrary, especially the mammoth skeletons he himself had helped to assemble. He wrote: "These great facts speak a universal language, and compel us to believe that there was a time when numbers of animals—and what is more extraordinary, larger animals than now remain—existed, had their day, and then perished. . . . The bones exist—the animals do not!"

When the essay was published, London's scientific community responded favorably to it. Sir Joseph Banks, a well-known explorer and naturalist, invited Rembrandt and Rubens to his breakfast gatherings and introduced them to many men of science, including the inventor of the steamboat, Robert Fulton. But the general public continued to stay away from the mammoth exhibit. In April 1803, six months after it opened, the Peales still owed more than $350 on the rent for the exhibition room.

By this time, even Rembrandt was getting discouraged. Contributing to his gloom was worrisome news from abroad. He and Rubens had planned to go on to France after the exhibition closed in London, and meet in Paris with Georges Cuvier, the eminent French scientist. Their father had written Cuvier about the skeleton, and the Frenchman was eager to see it. However, the brothers now learned the Paris trip might not be possible after all. Great Britain had declared war on France in May 1803, and travel between the two countries had become very risky.

Although they were still in debt, Rembrandt and Rubens closed the London exhibit in June 1803. They moved the mammoth skeleton to the small city of Reading, thirty-five miles west of London, and opened a new exhibition there in mid-July. The mayor of Reading gave them the free use of a room in the city hall to display the mammoth, and this helped them to make a modest profit on the exhibition. So did the ticket sales to flocks of schoolboys, who willingly spent their pocket money to gaze in awe at the mammoth's mighty tusks.

From Reading, the Peales took the skeleton on to the port city of Bristol. England's biggest fair was held there every September, and Rembrandt hoped the crowds who attended it would want to see the mammoth, too. Unfortunately, that didn't happen. After reading the posters and handbills, many potential visitors declared the skeleton must be a fake. Rembrandt was furious. "Even in the Borough of Bristol," he wrote, "they dare to suspect the bones were not made by the Creator of *my flesh* and *their flesh.*"

Before fall came, Rubens wrote their father that he and Rembrandt had "lost all hope of being able to visit Paris" because of the ongoing conflict between Great Britain and France. He added that Rembrandt was "heartily sick of traveling with the exhibition." The brothers cut their trip short in Bristol and returned home much sooner than planned. They arrived safely in Philadelphia with the mammoth skeleton on November 5.

A newspaper article made fun of Rembrandt's premature homecoming. "Perhaps Mr. Peale had heard of the voracious appetite of the French soldiers, and also of their recent invention of extracting soup from bones, and feared his precious skeleton might be stewed down into the kettle of 'bone soup' to refresh the French army."

Their father looked more favorably on his sons' early return, and on the results of their stay in England. He wrote a friend that the British exhibitions, while disappointing financially, had inspired "some professional men in London to make comparisons of the bones of various animals, which before they had no thought of." He added that Rembrandt was going to take the skeleton on a tour of American cities in hopes of recouping the losses incurred on the English trip.

The elder Peale had been busy while his sons were away. In 1802, after the federal government left Philadelphia for the new city of Washington, he moved most of his natural history museum into the empty rooms on the second floor of the statehouse. This is the building now known as Independence Hall. But the mammoth remained on display in its own special room at the American Philosophical Society.

In March 1804, Rembrandt took the second mammoth skeleton to Charleston, South Carolina. It was advertised as "the Great Aborigine of America"—*aborigine* means "earliest known inhabitant"—and drew large crowds during the month it was on exhibit. Later in 1804, Rembrandt displayed the skeleton to equally large crowds in Baltimore, Maryland. After these successful showings, he was able to pay off all the debts he and Rubens had amassed in England.

Ever since he had unearthed the mammoths, Charles Willson Peale had wanted to paint a picture of the great event. At last, in 1806, he began work on the painting. In December of that year, he wrote to a friend: "I have resumed my pencil and lately finished an historical picture of taking up the mammoth bones from a morass. It is a composition of between fifty and sixty figures, and by far the most important work that I have done."

[OVERLEAF] *The Exhumation of the Mammoth* (later, *The Exhumation of the Mastodon*), by Charles Willson Peale.
Courtesy of the Maryland Historical Society

Throughout 1806 and 1807, Peale kept on adding new figures to the painting, which was not completed until 1808. He titled it *The Exhumation of the Mammoth*. Besides portraits of Peale, his son Rembrandt, and the workers who had helped with the excavations, the canvas included pictures of many other people who had not taken part—Peale's wife Hannah, several of his other children, and various friends. Thus it ended up being as much a family portrait as an accurate picture of the exhumation.

Meanwhile, in 1806, Georges Cuvier had issued a surprising statement concerning the mammoth. The statement had a direct bearing on the Peales and their work, but they did not learn of it until two years later because of poor communications between France and America.

Cuvier had made a careful study of the casts of the mammoth bones and teeth that Charles Willson Peale had sent him. He had also read Rembrandt Peale's essays on the animal. Now he announced that the creature the Peales had unearthed combined features of the elephant and the hippopotamus, but was different from both. It differed, too, from the Siberian mammoth, which was more closely related to the elephant. In fact, the American discovery was not a mammoth at all, Cuvier said, but another kind of mammal entirely.

In his studies, Cuvier had paid special attention to the creature's unusual teeth. The domelike projections on them made him think of a woman's breasts. This gave Cuvier the idea for a name for the mysterious animal. He called it *mastodon*, from the Greek words for "breast" and "teeth," and that is the name by which it has been known ever since.

Cuvier's examination of the mastodon's teeth and bones led him to question several of Rembrandt's conclusions about the

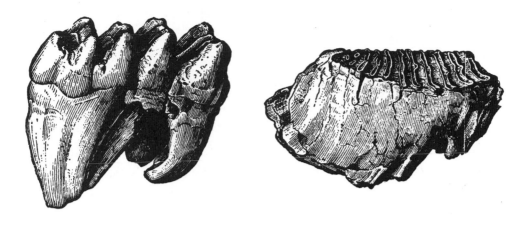

Comparative drawing of a mastodon tooth (left) and the tooth of a mammoth.
Neg. No. 410796, photo by H. S. Rice, courtesy Dept. of Library Services, American Museum of Natural History

animal. Unlike Peale, Cuvier decided the mastodon had fed on grasses and plants, not the flesh of other creatures. Cuvier also determined that the mastodon's tusks must have curved upward rather than downward. However, Cuvier agreed with Rembrandt that the animal was most definitely extinct. Overcoming his earlier hesitations, the French scientist wrote: "There is not the least proof, not the least bit of evidence, that the mastodon still lives in America or anywhere else."

This was the first time a respected scientist had openly acknowledged that a creature could become extinct. By saying so, and saying it firmly, Cuvier dealt a severe blow to those scientists and Bible scholars who sincerely believed that nothing God had created could ever die out.

But what could have killed off a powerful creature like the mastodon? Cuvier speculated that it must have been some great catastrophe—a devastating earthquake or a tremendous flood— that had wiped out many living things on Earth. It wasn't the Old

Testament deluge, though. Judging by the geological evidence, Cuvier concluded that this catastrophe had occurred much longer ago than Noah's flood.

When the Peales finally learned of Cuvier's statement, they felt as if all their efforts in digging up the mysterious bones and putting them together had been justified. Their finds had enabled the French scientist to identify the animal conclusively. They had also helped prove to him that it was extinct. Now the Peales had to get used to Cuvier's new name for the creature—*mastodon*.

CHAPTER 7

Even Bigger Giants

After Charles Willson Peale learned in 1808 that Cuvier had renamed the mammoth, he wrote his friend Thomas Jefferson and asked him what he thought of the creature's new name. Jefferson wrote back that *mastodon* seemed an acceptable choice. "It is more important that all should agree in giving the same name to the same thing," he said, "than that it should be the very best which might be given."

Feeling reassured, Peale changed the name on the label of the skeleton in his museum, and decided to give a christening party for the mastodon on July 4, 1809. He also changed the title of his painting of the creature's discovery. From then on, it was known as *The Exhumation of the Mastodon.*

In 1808, Rembrandt Peale had finally gotten his wish to go to Paris. He decided not to take the second mastodon skeleton with him because of the political situation in Europe, which remained unsettled. However, he did paint portraits of many French scholars and scientists, including Georges Cuvier. His father had written Cuvier that Rembrandt was coming. "I

Ticket of admission to Peale's Philadelphia museum, signed by Rubens Peale.
Courtesy American Philosophical Society

imagine you will have some pleasure in conversing with him [Rembrandt] on his and my joint labors in bringing to light the fantastic skeleton of so stupendous an animal as the mastodon," Peale said.

When he turned sixty-nine in 1810, Charles Willson Peale decided to hand over the management of his museum to his son Rubens. Peale planned to retire to a farm near Philadelphia, just as Thomas Jefferson had retired to his estate, Monticello, after leaving the presidency. But Peale maintained a keen interest in the affairs of the museum. In June 1811, for example, he helped Rubens take apart the mastodon skeleton and transport it to spacious new quarters in the statehouse.

Rembrandt Peale moved to Baltimore in 1812 and opened a

museum of his own in that city, which was then the third largest in the United States. He took the other mastodon skeleton with him and put it on display in the new museum. To show his support for his son, Charles Willson Peale willed the skeleton to Rembrandt in 1818 so that it might always be a part of his Baltimore museum.

In the meantime, the remains of other mysterious creatures were being discovered—creatures even bigger and stranger than the mastodon. An eleven-year-old girl, Mary Anning, saw some bones protruding from a cliff while walking with her brother along the beach at Lyme Regis in southern England in 1810. The two young people chipped away at the rocks with hammers and chisels until they uncovered the outline of a skeleton almost thirty feet long. The monstrous creature had four flippers, and jaws filled with sharply pointed teeth. Scientists who examined the find said it was the skeleton of an extinct marine reptile. They called it an *Ichthyosaurus*, from the Greek words for "fish" and "lizard."

Fossil of an *Ichthyosaurus*.

Neg. No. 313168, photo by H. S. Rice, courtesy Dept. of Library Services, American Museum of Natural History

The remains of an even larger creature were found in 1821 by an English physician and fossil hunter, Dr. Gideon Algernon Mantell. Deep in a quarry in Cuckfield, England, north of Brighton, Dr. Mantell discovered six enormous teeth and several unusual bones. The teeth were so big that Dr. Mantell decided they must come from an animal at least fifty feet long. He had no idea what the creature might be, so he arranged to have one of the teeth taken to Georges Cuvier in Paris for identification.

Cuvier disappointed Mantell by declaring that the tooth came from a rhinoceros. Unconvinced, Mantell sent the French scientist some of the creature's fossilized bones. These, Cuvier said, belonged to a species of hippopotamus. Mantell was still not ready to accept the French expert's verdicts. The doctor took the teeth and bones to a museum in London, where a researcher noted a strong resemblance between the fossilized teeth and those of the iguana, a lizard found in Central America.

Mantell was now convinced that he had discovered the teeth and bones of a huge lizard. He gave it the name *Iguanodon*, meaning "iguana tooth," and in 1825 he presented a full report on the creature to the Royal Society in London. Long ages ago, Mantell said, lizards far larger than any known today must have roamed the Earth.

When Cuvier read Mantell's report, filled with details of the evidence he had gathered, the French scientist realized that he had been mistaken in his earlier judgments. He agreed with Mantell that the remains the English doctor had found were those of an extinct, plant-eating reptile.

[RIGHT] Drawing of an *Iguanodon*, based on studies of the creature's skeleton.
Neg. No. 330036, photo by Rota, courtesy Dept. of Library Services, American Museum of Natural History

In the next few years, the bones of other giant reptiles were found at various places in England. So many had been discovered by 1841 that a British scientist, Sir Richard Owen, suggested they be given a family name. He proposed that the creatures be called *dinosauria*, which means "fearfully great lizards" in Greek. Scientists and the general public soon adopted the new name, but over time they anglicized it to the one we know today—*dinosaurs*.

While fresh discoveries of dinosaur bones were being made, geologists were advancing new theories about the Earth's age and its history. These theories did not rule out the possibility of a divine creation, but they said it must have occurred much earlier than the Bible indicated. Nor did they deny Cuvier's notion that the Earth's history had been shaped by a series of catastrophes like the flood described in Genesis. But based on a careful study of the layers in rock formations, the geologists concluded that the Earth was far older than anyone had heretofore imagined.

One of the most widely accepted of the new theories was known as "uniformitarianism." It put forth the idea that all the features of the Earth—its mountains, oceans, vegetation, and animal life—were the result of constant but gradual change. According to this theory, the Earth as we know it was not the product of any single act of creation, or devastating catastrophe, but rather of developments that had taken place over uncounted millions of years. A supporter of this theory, James Hutton, wrote that in the Earth's history "we find no vestige of a beginning,—no prospect of an end."

Another scientist, Charles Darwin, took the notion of seemingly endless time and constructed his own theory to explain how and why the Earth had changed over the ages. This is the theory of evolution, which is still a subject of controversy today, a century and a half after Darwin first proposed it.

According to Darwin's theory, new forms of life descend from older forms in the course of time. For example, some reptiles may have evolved into birds; some apes may have developed into humans. This pattern of change—this evolution—is hastened by what Darwin called the process of natural selection. Those organisms that prove to be the best adapted to their environment will survive and produce offspring. Those that do not adapt well will die.

Where did the dinosaurs fit into these various theories about the Earth and its history? After studying the rock strata in which different fossils were found, nineteenth-century scientists worked out the geologic time scale that is still used today. The scientists could not then tell exactly when each period on the time scale began and ended, but they knew that most of the dinosaurs whose fossils they had identified lived during the Triassic, Jurassic, and Cretaceous periods.

Today, a clearer picture of the time scale can be obtained through radioactive, or radiometric, dating. In this process, scientists estimate the age of a rock layer by measuring, against known rates, the radioactive decay of uranium and other elements found within the rock. Aided by such dating, scientists can now say with confidence that the Triassic period began at least 230 million years ago, and the Cretaceous period came to an end 65 million years ago. Thus the dinosaurs strode the Earth for at least 165 million years.

By comparison, the mastodon is only a baby in terms of its place on the geologic time scale. It lived during the two most recent epochs—the Pleistocene, which began approximately

G E O L O G I C   T I M E   S C A L E

Era	Period	Epoch	Biological Forms	Years Before the Present
Cenozoic	Quaternary	Holocene (recent)		
				11,000
		Pleistocene (glacial)	Earliest humans	
				500,000–2 million
	Tertiary	Pliocene		
				12 million
		Miocene	Earliest hominids	
				25 million
		Oligocene		
				36 million
		Eocene		
				58 million
		Paleocene	Earliest large mammals	
				65 million
Mesozoic	Cretaceous		Dinosaurs in ascendance	
				135 million
	Jurassic		Earliest birds and mammals	
				180 million
	Triassic		Age of Dinosaurs begins	
				230 million
Paleozoic	Permian			
				280 million
	Upper Carboniferous (Pennsylvanian)		Earliest reptiles	
				310 million
	Lower Carboniferous (Mississippian)		Earliest winged insects	
				345 million
	Devonian		Earliest amphibians	
				405 million
	Silurian		Earliest insects	
				425 million
	Ordovician		Earliest corals	
				500 million
	Cambrian		Earliest fish	
				600 million

2 million years ago, and the Holocene, which followed the Pleistocene about 11,000 years ago and is the period we are in today. Radioactive dating of mastodon remains indicates that the animal was still alive as recently as 11,000 years ago. At that time, early people were already settled in North America.

Even though he had unearthed its remains, Charles Willson Peale did not know these basic facts about the mastodon when he died in February 1827, at the age of eighty-five. They would be left for later scientists to discover. Unfortunately, those scientists would not have the benefit of studying the mastodon skeleton that Peale had worked so hard to assemble. It was taken apart after his Philadelphia museum closed, twenty years after his death, and the bones were sold to various institutions and individuals.

The other mastodon skeleton had a happier fate. When Rembrandt Peale retired from his Baltimore museum, he sold the skeleton to the famous showman P. T. Barnum, who displayed it in his museum in New York City. Eventually, the skeleton reached Europe, where it was bought in 1854 by a museum in the German city of Darmstadt. The skeleton survived the Allied air raids that destroyed most of Darmstadt in World War II. Today it can still be seen there, as impressive as when the Peales first set it up in Philadelphia.

In the light of later discoveries, it would be easy to overlook or underestimate the Peales' scientific accomplishments. But without the proof of the mastodon skeletons they unearthed, scientists like Georges Cuvier might not have been as ready to accept the idea of extinction. Or to revise their notions about the age and history of the Earth.

The mastodon skeletons helped to lay the groundwork for a new understanding of the Earth and its creatures, and the long road both have traveled through the ages. Many stretches of that road remain to be explored. Many gaps in our knowledge of plant and animal development, including our own development, remain to be filled.

It will be no easy task for future scientists to fill in these gaps. But as they go about their work, they can draw inspiration from the pioneering scientists of the past—far-seeing people like Charles Willson Peale and his son Rembrandt.

[LEFT] Skeleton of mastodon discovered by Charles Willson Peale.
Photo by Werner Kumpf, courtesy Hessisches Landesmuseum, Darmstadt

BEYOND THE MYSTERY . . .

More About
Charles Willson Peale

Like his friends Thomas Jefferson and Benjamin Franklin, Charles Willson Peale was a man of many talents. At different times in his life—and often at the same time—Peale painted portraits, operated a museum, invented useful devices, and led scientific expeditions such as the unearthing of the mastodon.

Peale, who was born in Annapolis, Maryland, in 1741, did not have an easy start in life. His father, a schoolteacher, died when Charles was eight, leaving almost nothing to his widow and four young children. Mrs. Peale managed to support the family by making dresses for well-to-do women. She sent young Charles to a charity school, where he showed a natural talent for drawing. But he had to give up school at the age of thirteen after he was apprenticed to a man who made and repaired saddles.

When Charles was eighteen, he fell in love with a pretty girl of fifteen, Rachel Brewer. She was not interested in him at first, but later changed her mind. At twenty, Peale won an early release from his apprenticeship because of his steady, careful work. He borrowed money from his former master, set himself up as an independent saddler, and married his young love, Rachel.

To make more money and repay his loan, Charles studied other trades in his spare time. He learned upholstering, clock- and watchmaking, and silversmithing, and practiced them along with saddle making. It didn't seem unusual for someone like Peale to teach himself so many different skills. All of America was still a frontier in the last years of the eighteenth century, and few people had any specialized training in their occupations.

Peale also taught himself how to paint pictures in watercolors and oils, and began to make portraits of his friends and neighbors. Portrait painting was a lucrative business in the days before the camera was invented. To perfect his talents, Peale persuaded an established artist to let him watch while the man painted an oil portrait. In return, Peale promised to give him one of his best saddles. The artist sketched in the outline of the subject's face and painted one side of it. Then he let Peale paint the other side so that the young beginner might gain experience.

On a trip to Boston, Peale met the well-known artist John Singleton Copley, who advised him to concentrate on miniature portraits. There was a great demand then for pictures of loved ones that were small enough to be put in lockets. Back home in Maryland, Peale established such a strong reputation as a portraitist that his wealthy patrons offered to send him to England for further training. In London, he studied with Benjamin West, an American artist who had emigrated from the colonies to England. But being in London only reinforced Peale's loyalties to his native land. When King George III passed by in his carriage one day, Peale refused to take off his hat.

Peale returned to America in 1769 and quickly became one of the

Charles Willson Peale as an art student in London. *Portrait by Benjamin West, 1767–69.*

© Collection of The New-York Historical Society

best-known portrait painters in the colonies. In 1772, he was summoned to Mount Vernon to paint the first full-scale portrait of a gentleman farmer and militia colonel named George Washington. At the same time, Peale painted a miniature of Washington's wife, Martha.

In June 1776, Peale and his family settled in Philadelphia, the city that was to be his home for most of the rest of his life. During the Revolutionary War, Peale served as a lieutenant in the militia and took part in the battle of Princeton. He looked out for his men, procured whatever food was available for them, and made them leather moccasins with his own hands. Those under him respected Peale so much that they elected him captain.

That winter at Valley Forge, Peale painted miniatures of forty officers for them to send back to their families. He also painted several more portraits of General Washington. After the fighting ended in victory for America, Peale was so popular that he could probably have become one of the leaders of the new nation. But he disliked politics and chose instead to go home to Philadelphia and resume his career as an artist. He enlarged upon the miniatures that he had made during the war and displayed the full-size paintings in a room in his home. Called the "Gallery of Great Men," it was the first art gallery in America.

A few years later, in 1786, Peale expanded his gallery into a "repository of natural curiosities." Thus began the first natural history museum in America, and one of the first in the world. Friends donated specimens of animals and birds to the museum, and Peale became an ardent collector himself. He also learned a new skill, taxidermy, so that he could prepare, stuff, and mount the specimens he acquired for the museum.

In 1790, Peale's wife Rachel died as a result of complications during her eleventh pregnancy. Of their ten other children, six—four sons and two daughters—lived to maturity. All of them were given the names of famous artists: Rembrandt, Rubens, Raphael, Angelica

[RIGHT] *The Artist in His Museum*, painting by Charles Willson Peale, 1822.
Courtesy The Pennsylvania Academy of the Fine Arts, Philadelphia.
Gift of Mrs. Sarah Harrison (The Joseph Harrison, Jr. Collection)

Kauffmann, etc. Their father had found the names in a book called Dictionary of Painters.

Soon after Rachel's death, Peale set out in search of a new wife to be his companion and serve as a mother to his children. He found her in the person of Elizabeth DePeyster, a young woman half his age—Peale was fifty when he married her, and she was twenty-five. Elizabeth bore him six more children, five of whom lived. Peale named the sons of this marriage for scientists: Charles Linnaeus and Benjamin Franklin. This reflected his growing interest in science, which had led him to open his natural history museum.

As Peale became more and more involved with running the museum, he decided to retire from portrait painting and leave the field to his artist sons, Rembrandt and Raphael. Then, in 1801, he undertook what was to be the most exciting adventure of his life—the unearthing of the mastodon.

After the death of Elizabeth DePeyster Peale in 1804, Peale married for a third time. His bride was Hannah Moore, a quiet Quaker lady closer to his own age. The Peales retired to a farm outside Philadelphia, but later decided to return to the city. Peale took up painting again and became actively involved with the museum once more.

In his spare time, Peale enjoyed working on various inventions. In 1819, he developed a machine known as a velocipede—a sort of bicycle without pedals. Although he was seventy-eight, Peale tried it out himself, riding in circles around his backyard. He also sought a more efficient type of false teeth, and hit upon making them out of porcelain. It proved to be a far better material for teeth than the ivory that had been commonly used up to then.

Peale's third wife, Hannah, died during a yellow-fever epidemic in 1821. The artist grieved for her but was not yet ready to give up on

Drawing of a velocipede (also known as a "pedestrian's hobby horse")
by Charles Willson Peale.
Courtesy American Philosophical Society

life. In 1827, at the age of eighty-six, he traveled to New York in search of a fourth wife. Unsuccessful in his quest, he was on his way home to Philadelphia when his ship ran aground near the landing place.

Despite warnings to take it easy, Peale grabbed his heavy trunk, slung it over his shoulder, and walked ashore. The strain was too much for his heart. When he finally reached Philadelphia, he took to his bed and rarely got up after that. On February 27, 1827, he awoke feeling extremely weak, and later that day he died. Thus ended the long, full life of a remarkably gifted human being: Charles Willson Peale.

The Fate of the
Mammoth and Mastodon

Today, the African elephant is the largest living land mammal. African bull elephants may reach a shoulder height of thirteen feet and weigh six to eight tons. But two of the elephant's extinct relatives, the mammoth and the mastodon, were just as large, or even larger. The steppe mammoth that ranged over Europe's grasslands 600,000 years ago was the largest of all mammoths. Adult males attained heights of more than fourteen feet at the shoulder and weighed at least ten tons.

The mammoth originated in the jungle woodlands of Africa and later migrated into Europe and the far-northern regions of Siberia. Eventually it reached North America, probably traveling over the same now-vanished land bridge between Siberia and Alaska that the first human settlers in North America used. Like the elephant, the mammoth ate the leaves, fruit, and bark of trees and shrubs, but its main food was grass. It had a large, single-domed head and long, curving tusks. One mammoth tusk found in Russia was sixteen and a half feet long—half again as long as the longest known elephant tusk.

African elephants.

Neg. No. 335194, photo by J. Thorpe, courtesy Dept. of Library Services, American Museum of Natural History

When the northern latitudes of the Earth became colder during the Ice Ages, mammoths living in those regions adapted by growing long, thick coats of fur that kept them warm. These hairy animals evolved into what we call woolly mammoths. They had their heyday during the last Ice Age, about 50,000 years ago, when glacier ice reached as far south as Holland in Europe and below the Great Lakes in North America. At that time, the woolly mammoths' range extended all the way from Ireland, across the top of Europe, Asia, Alaska, and Canada, and on to the east coast of North America.

South of the ice sheet in North America lived the Columbian mammoth, which was almost as big as its ancestor, the steppe mammoth. Adult Columbian males often reached a height of thirteen feet and weighed more than nine tons—the equivalent of 120 adult humans. Their curving tusks were just as impressive, too, averaging eleven or twelve feet in length. The main difference between the Columbian mammoth and the woolly mammoth was its coat, which was not as heavy or thick.

Like the elephant and the mammoth, the mastodon originated in Africa between 40 and 30 million years ago. The first mastodons were about four and a half feet high and had an extremely long jaw and no less than four tusks.

The mastodons of the Miocene epoch, between 25 and 12 million years ago, were the size of large elephants. These bigger mastodons had long, flexible trunks like those of elephants, and only two tusks. During this period, the mastodons branched out from their African base and migrated in large numbers to Europe, Asia, and North America.

The remains of two types of mastodons have been found at various sites in North America. The shovel tusker mastodon, fossils of

A Columbian mammoth, as painted by Charles R. Knight.

Neg. No. 328176, photo by Logan, courtesy Dept. of Library Services, American Museum of Natural History

which have been discovered in Nebraska, had four-foot-long tusks and a lower jaw that reached the incredible length of seven feet! The jaw looked like a huge scoop, and that's probably how the mastodon used it, shoving back into its mouth plants that its trunk had yanked out of the ground.

The more common mastodon found in what is now the United States was the true or American mastodon. This was the animal whose bones Charles Willson Peale dug up near Newburgh, New York. Somewhat smaller than today's African elephant, the American mastodon averaged ten feet in height at the shoulder and was about fifteen feet long from the base of the tusks to the start of the tail. Like the elephant and the mammoth, the American mastodon enjoyed a long life. Most mastodons had a life span of between sixty and seventy years, and some reached the age of eighty.

The American mastodon was a forest dweller that obtained most of its food by browsing among trees and shrubs. As we have seen, it had unusual, breast-shaped teeth, which distinguished it from both the elephant and the mammoth. Another major difference was the structure of its head. Unlike the skulls of the elephant and the mammoth, that of the mastodon was relatively flat on top. The mastodon also carried its head horizontally, while the heads of the elephant and mammoth assumed a more vertical position.

Fossil bones of the American mastodon are so common, especially in the eastern United States, that scientists think the animal once roamed the North American continent in enormous numbers. Some believe the mastodon herds equaled or outnumbered the herds of bison that filled the Great Plains before nineteenth-century white hunters and sportsmen wiped them out. Fossils of more than a hundred mastodons have been found at one Kentucky site alone. This was Big Bone Lick, the place from which the fossil bones came that Charles Willson Peale drew . . . the bones that aroused his interest in the mastodon.

When the first humans migrated from Asia to North America about 13,000 years ago, they no doubt saw vast herds of mammoths and mastodons spread out on the grassy plains and feeding amid the trees. Two thousand years later—a mere blink in geological time—

A family of mastodons in a marsh, from a painting by Charles R. Knight.

Neg. No. 32528, photo by Kay C. Lenskjold, courtesy Dept. of Library Services, American Museum of Natural History

almost all the huge animals had vanished from the Earth. What caused them to disappear? This is the question that continues to vex scientists as they attempt to find the reason for one of the biggest extinctions in history.

Some scientists think the drastic changes in climate that occurred at the end of the last Ice Age were to blame. As the temperature grew warmer, forests advanced, replacing the areas of grass and woodland that the mammoths and mastodons depended on for food.

An adult Columbian mammoth needed more than two hundred pounds of fresh food a day to fuel its bulk, and probably spent most of its waking hours in the search for edible shrubs, plants, and grasses. The somewhat smaller mastodon required almost as much food. If the huge animals' sources of supply were sharply reduced, they soon would have fallen victim to starvation.

But would that have been enough to cause their complete extinction? Many scientists doubt it, arguing that the mammoths and mastodons had survived equally severe climatic changes in earlier Ice Ages. These scientists believe that it was human beings, armed with improved spears and other weapons, who were responsible for the extinction of the animals. We know from their cave paintings, and from fossil finds near their settlements, that early peoples hunted the mammoth and mastodon. They ate the creatures' flesh, carved their tusks into tools and weapons, and used mammoth bones in the construction of shelters.

In time, steady hunting would have brought about a steep decline in the animals' population because of their slow reproduction rate. Mammoths and mastodons mated in the late spring and had only one offspring at a time. The gestation period was twenty-two months—the longest for any mammal. At birth, a baby mammoth stood three and a half feet tall and weighed about two hundred pounds, and a baby mastodon was almost as big. Then it took the animals at least fifteen years to reach maturity and be able to produce young of their own.

Strong support for the theory that hunting by humans caused the animals' extinction seems to come from North America. There, the mammoth and mastodon thrived until the arrival of the first people. A few centuries later, both creatures had disappeared entirely. But could a small number of humans, scattered over a vast continent, really have wiped out the sprawling herds of mammoths and mastodons? There is little fossil evidence to indicate that early Americans engaged in the sort of big-game hunts that would have resulted in such mass destruction.

Recently a different explanation for the animals' extinction has won the support of many scientists. They believe the mammoths and mastodons were struck by some new and deadly epidemic disease. What could this disease have been? The scientists don't yet know, but they speculate it was carried by dogs, rats, birds, or other living baggage that accompanied the first humans to North America. Or perhaps it was brought by the humans themselves.

The humans and other carriers would have learned to live with the agent that caused the disease. But the immune systems of the mammoths and mastodons would have had no previous experience with it, and thus would have been utterly defenseless when the agent infected them. The disease would have spread rapidly through the mammoth and mastodon herds, affecting all the animals from the youngest to the oldest. Their population would have been reduced so sharply that the animals would have been unable to replenish their numbers before a new epidemic hit them. Within a relatively short time, they would have been driven to extinction.

Scientists think the rabies virus might have been the guilty party, or a type of leptospirosis, a bacterium spread in rat urine. Or it might have been a disease that is completely unknown today. In search of the answer, the scientists plan to test the mummified remains of mammoths and other animals from the Pleistocene epoch to see if there are traces of disease organisms in their bodies.

Comparative drawing of a mastodon (left) and a mammoth (right).
Neg. No. 329040, courtesy Dept. of Library Services, American Museum of Natural History

Perhaps no single explanation can account for the extinction of the mammoths and mastodons. It may have been due instead to a combination of factors. Weather changes at the end of the Ice Age probably reduced the food supply and led to the deaths of the more vulnerable animals—the sick, the injured, the youngest, and the oldest. Overhunting by humans could have caused the mammoth and mastodon populations to drop still further. Then, if a new and fatal epidemic disease struck, the stage would have been set for the complete extinction of the animals.

The Fate of the Mammoth and Mastodon

Like the disappearance of the dinosaurs, the extinction of the mammoths and mastodons remains a mystery. Only through further scientific investigations can we hope to discover what actually happened to these and other creatures that vanished from the Earth in the distant past.

Bibliography
and Source Notes

My interest in Charles Willson Peale began with an exhibition of his art that I saw at the Metropolitan Museum of Art in New York City in 1982. Intrigued by the paintings on display and wanting to know more about Peale, I bought the exhibition catalogue, *Charles Willson Peale and His World* by Edgar P. Richardson, Brook Hindle, and Lillian B. Miller (New York: Harry N. Abrams, 1982).

A brief portion of the catalogue described how Peale had excavated and assembled the first mastodon skeleton. This sounded as if it had the makings of an exciting true story for young people, but the telling in the catalogue was too sketchy to form the basis of a full-length book. Since I was busy at the time with several other writing projects, I put the idea aside. I didn't discard it, though— merely stored it in my memory.

The idea resurfaced fifteen years later, in 1997, when I discovered that a detailed account of the excavation was included in a scholarly work that had recently been acquired by The New York Public Library: *The Selected Papers of Charles Willson Peale and His Family*, Volumes 1–4, Lillian B. Miller, editor (New Haven: Yale University Press, 1983). In Volume 2, Part 1 of the papers, I was delighted to find Peale's own chronicle of the expedition, told through his letters and excerpts from his diaries. The bulk of *The Mystery of the Mammoth*

Bones has been drawn from these letters and diary entries, and all the quotations attributed to Peale come from them.

Another important source of firsthand information was his son Rembrandt Peale's *An Historical Disquisition on the Mammoth, or, a Great American Incognitum, an Extinct Immense, Carnivorous Animal Whose Fossil Remains Have Been Found in North America* (London, 1803). In this essay, Rembrandt offers his version of the key events that occurred during the expedition and presents a summary of his and his father's findings concerning the mammoth.

Material on Rembrandt and his brother Rubens' trip to England with the second mammoth skeleton, and the quotations attributed to the two brothers, also come from Volume 2, Part 1 of the Peale family's *Selected Papers*. The information about Rembrandt's tour of the eastern United States with the second skeleton, his journey to Paris in 1808, and Charles Willson Peale's painting *The Exhumation of the Mastodon* was located in Volume 2, Part 2. Details of Rembrandt's founding of the Peale Museum in Baltimore and his father's willing the second skeleton to him were taken from Volume 3.

Additional information on the life of Charles Willson Peale comes from the chapter devoted to Peale in *America's Old Masters* by James Thomas Flexner (Revised edition: Garden City, NY: Doubleday, 1980; New York: McGraw-Hill, 1982). Another valuable resource was a biography written for young people, *The Ingenious Mr. Peale: Painter, Patriot, and Man of Science* by Janet Wilson (New York: Atheneum Books for Young Readers, 1996).

The following books were primary sources for information on other topics discussed in *The Mystery of the Mammoth Bones*:

THEORIES ABOUT THE AGE OF THE EARTH

Evolution: The History of an Idea by Peter J. Bowler (Berkeley and Los Angeles: University of California Press, 1983); *Charles Darwin: A New Life* by John Bowlby (New York and London: W. W. Norton, 1991); and *The Riddle of the Dinosaur* by John Noble Wilford (New York: Alfred A. Knopf, 1985).

ICHTHYOSAURUS, IGUANODON, AND OTHER EARLY DINOSAURS

Again, *The Riddle of the Dinosaur* by Wilford.

Bibliography and Source Notes

MAMMOTHS AND MASTODONS

The Age of Great Mammals by Daniel Cohen (New York: Dodd, Mead, 1969); *Mammoths* by Adrian Lister and Paul Bahn (New York: Macmillan, 1994); and a magazine article, "Mammoth Site," by Larry D. Agenbroad, in *Natural History*, October 1997.

THE NATIVE AMERICAN TRADITION ABOUT THE MAMMOTH

The Portable Thomas Jefferson, edited and with an introduction by Merrill D. Peterson (New York: Viking Penguin, 1975); and *An Historical Disquisition on the Mammoth* by Rembrandt Peale.

—J.C.G.
February 1998

Index

Index

JAMES CROSS GIBLIN knew he was onto something when he found a detailed account of the unearthing of the mastodon in Charles Willson Peale's diaries and letters. "This true story had everything: drama, suspense, and the search for a gigantic, unknown beast," he says. "But beyond that, I was fascinated by the details of life in 1801 that Peale's writings contained—how long it took to travel from Philadelphia to New York City; what Peale and his workers ate for dinner; etc. How different everyday life was then—and yet how similar when it came to people's feelings and needs."

Mr. Giblin is the author of eighteen books for young readers, many of which have won awards and honors. Twelve of his titles, most recently *Charles A. Lindbergh: A Human Hero* and *When Plague Strikes: The Black Death, Smallpox, AIDS*, have been named Notable Children's Books by the American Library Association. In 1996 he received the *Washington Post*–Children's Book Guild Award for Nonfiction for his body of work. Mr. Giblin lives in New York City.